Put Beginning Readers on the Right Track with
ALL ABOARD READING™

The All Aboard Reading series is especially designed for beginning readers. Written by noted authors and illustrated in full color, these are books that children really want to read—books to excite their imagination, expand their interests, make them laugh, and support their feelings. With fiction and nonfiction stories that are high interest and curriculum-related, All Aboard Reading books offer something for every young reader. And with four different reading levels, the All Aboard Reading series lets you choose which books are most appropriate for your children and their growing abilities.

Picture Readers
Picture Readers have super-simple texts, with many nouns appearing as rebus pictures. At the end of each book are 24 flash cards—on one side is a rebus picture; on the other side is the written-out word.

Station Stop 1
Station Stop 1 books are best for children who have just begun to read. Simple words and big type make these early reading experiences more comfortable. Picture clues help children to figure out the words on the page. [. . . repetition . . .] the text helps children to predict the next word [. . .] oping word recognition.

Station Stop 2
Station Stop 2 books are written specifically for [. . .]ng with help. Short sentences make it easier for early reader [. . .]and what they are reading. Simple plots and simple dialogue help children with reading comprehension.

Station Stop 3
Station Stop 3 books are perfect for children who are reading alone. With longer text and harder words, these books appeal to children who have mastered basic reading skills. More complex stories captivate children who are ready for more challenging books.

More books by Ginjer L. Clarke

All Aboard Science Reader: Bug Out! The World's Creepiest, Crawliest Critters

All Aboard Science Reader: Freak Out! Animals Beyond Your Wildest Imagination

All Aboard Science Reader: Gross Out! Animals That Do Disgusting Things

All Aboard Science Reader: Fake Out! Animals That Play Tricks

All Aboard Science Reader: Black Out!: Animals that Live in the Dark

For all of my curious young readers,
who love weird, wonderful animals
as much as I do.—G.L.C.

In memory of Elizabeth W. Mueller.
She was pretty amazing herself.—P.M.

GROSSET & DUNLAP
Published by the Penguin Group
Penguin Group (USA) Inc., 375 Hudson Street, New York, New York 10014, USA
Penguin Group (Canada), 90 Eglinton Avenue East, Suite 700,
Toronto, Ontario M4P 2Y3, Canada
(a division of Pearson Penguin Canada Inc.)
Penguin Books Ltd., 80 Strand, London WC2R 0RL, England
Penguin Group Ireland, 25 St. Stephen's Green, Dublin 2, Ireland
(a division of Penguin Books Ltd.)
Penguin Group (Australia), 250 Camberwell Road, Camberwell, Victoria 3124, Australia
(a division of Pearson Australia Group Pty. Ltd.)
Penguin Books India Pvt. Ltd., 11 Community Centre, Panchsheel Park,
New Delhi—110 017, India
Penguin Group (NZ), 67 Apollo Drive, Rosedale, North Shore 0632, New Zealand
(a division of Pearson New Zealand Ltd.)
Penguin Books (South Africa) (Pty.) Ltd., 24 Sturdee Avenue,
Rosebank, Johannesburg 2196, South Africa

Penguin Books Ltd., Registered Offices: 80 Strand, London WC2R 0RL, England

Text copyright © 2009 by Ginjer L. Clarke. Illustrations copyright © 2009 by Pete Mueller. All
rights reserved. Published by Grosset & Dunlap, a division of Penguin Young Readers Group,
345 Hudson Street, New York, New York 10014. ALL ABOARD SCIENCE READER and
GROSSET & DUNLAP are trademarks of Penguin Group (USA) Inc. Printed in the U.S.A.

Library of Congress Control Number: 2008048134

ISBN 978-0-448-44826-8   10 9 8 7 6 5 4 3 2 1

FAR OUT!
Animals That Do Amazing Things

By Ginjer L. Clarke
Illustrated by Pete Mueller

Grosset & Dunlap

Do you ever wonder

if animals can talk?

Many animals make noises

in the same way that people talk.

They show anger, fear, surprise,

worry, love, and happiness—

just like we do with our voices.

Other animals act like
humans in different ways.
Some use tools, have jobs,
and can remember things.
Let's find out what these
amazing animals can do!

Chapter 1

Animals That Communicate

What animal is the smartest?

Many scientists think dolphins are.

They have the biggest brains

of all animals other than humans

for the size of their bodies.

Dolphins can learn things like we do.

Dolphins communicate, or talk,

using clicks and whistles

and many other sounds underwater.

This is called echolocation

(say: eh-co-lo-KAY-shun).

Creeaak! Creeaak!

These **bottlenose dolphins** use
their sounds to work together.
They swim fast around a
huge school, or group, of fish.
They need to communicate to go in
the same direction and the same speed.
Hundreds of dolphins form a type of
net to catch the fish and eat them.

Some **orcas** can learn tricks
from animal trainers.
But in the wild, orcas are called
killer whales because they
are fast, fierce hunters.
Orcas eat many animals,
including squid, birds, turtles,
seals, sharks, and other whales.

These orcas are hunting together.

Each group, or pod, of orcas

uses different noises to talk.

They communicate with a

language of their own that

other orcas do not understand.

This special way of talking

helps the pod work together.

Whoosh! One orca spots a penguin,

and they all attack quickly.

Ca-caaw!

In the forests of Australia
lives an odd, noisy bird.
The **superb lyrebird** is about
the size of a chicken.
It spreads out its fancy tail
like a peacock to look larger.
Lyrebirds usually hide in trees,
but they have a lot to say.

These lyrebirds talk to one another
using many different songs.
They can also mimic, or pretend
to sound like, other birds.
They probably do this
to charm other birds.
The bird who sings
the most beautiful song
gets the most attention in the forest.

The **siamang gibbon**

(say: SEE-uh-mang GIB-en)

lives in the Malaysian rain forest.

Gibbons are small apes that can

swing through the treetops.

They have superlong arms.

They are one of a few primates that

can walk standing up like humans.

Hooo-OO! Hooo-OO!

This male gibbon puffs out
his throat sac and hoots loudly.
His call can be heard from far away.
Gibbon families sing together
and compete with other groups
to see who is the loudest.
Their barks and yells help them
find one another in the forest.

Have you ever seen a gorilla

up close at a zoo?

They look and act a lot like people do.

Some gorillas have learned

to talk using sign language!

But they have their own

language in the jungle.

This big, male **silverback gorilla**
is angry at a young, male gorilla.
He uses his body and voice
to say, "Go away!"
He stands and pounds his chest.
Then he barks, growls, and
shows his sharp, pointed teeth.
All of the gorillas listen
when this amazing ape talks.

Chapter 2

Animals That Use Tools

Chimpanzees say a lot, too.

Some use their hands to talk.

A few famous chimps have learned

hundreds of words in sign language.

They have also learned how

to use tools just like we do.

Chimps can use sticks to get
honey from a hive, dig up roots,
and even escape from cages.
This hungry chimp pokes a stick
into a termite mound and pulls it out.
She holds the stick in both hands.
Slurp! The chimp quickly licks
the termites off the stick.
She made an insect Popsicle!

The **woodpecker finch**

does not have any hands.

But it uses tools to find bugs, too.

This bird has a short tongue

that cannot reach into

deep holes in tree branches.

So when it wants to get at

bugs that are hiding, it uses

a tool to make its tongue longer.

This finch uses its beak to
break a spine off a cactus.
It jabs the spine into a branch
and catches a juicy grub worm.
Chomp! It munches the worm.
The finch holds the spine
in its foot to use again later.

The **Egyptian vulture** knows

how to get the food it wants.

Big ostrich eggs are tasty.

But they are harder to crack

than smaller eggs.

Other birds throw big eggs on the ground

until they break open.

But that takes a long time.

This vulture wants food now!

It finds a big rock nearby

and picks it up in its beak.

Crash! Smash!

It cracks the egg with the rock.

The egg breaks open, and

the vulture gobbles up his dinner.

Sea otters live in the water almost all of the time. They have to dive down in the ocean to find food. But a clam is hard to open. What will the otter do? She grabs a clam and a flat rock with her front feet.

Then she puts the rock on her belly
and smashes the shell on the rock.
Craacck! The shell pops open.
She slurps the soft clam inside.
Otters can break crabs and other
hard sea creatures like this, too.

Many monkeys learn quickly
when people show them
how to do something.
But **capuchin monkeys**
(say: ka-PYU-shen)
can learn to use tools
even in the wild.
Capuchin monkeys use rocks
to dig in the dirt for bugs and
to crack open nuts and seeds.

This capuchin monkey sets a
hard palm nut on a flat rock.
Then it picks up another rock
that is almost too heavy to hold.
Whack! The monkey bangs
the rock like a hammer
and cracks the nut.
What a clever capuchin!

Chapter 3

Animals That Have Jobs

Camels are important to people
in the deserts of Asia and Africa.
They carry heavy loads for *nomads*.
Nomads are people who walk
for many miles to move from
one place to another.
Camels also pull plows in fields
and turn wheels to water crops.

These **dromedary camels**

(say: DRA-meh-DARE-ee)

are walking in the Sahara desert

with a group of nomads.

They do not mind the heat and

can go a long time without water.

When the camels do find water,

they can drink up to thirty gallons.

That is almost a bathtub full!

Siberian huskies help people carry things just like camels— but in the snow, not the desert. Huskies have worked in Alaska for more than 100 years. They work in teams to pull heavy sleds and herd reindeer. Huskies were even used by Admiral Byrd to help him explore the South Pole.

This team of huskies is carrying
a sled full of supplies and medicine.
They zoom over the snowy trail.
Mush! Mush! calls their driver.
The dogs work together and listen
when their driver asks them
to change direction or speed.
Now it is time for their dinner
after a job well done.

German shepherd dogs

have lots of useful jobs.

Their first job a long time ago

was to herd sheep.

Today they are also rescue dogs,

police dogs, guide dogs,

hunting dogs, and show dogs.

They are very friendly animals.

But they get serious

when there is work to do.

This German shepherd sniffs
the air for a lost hiker.

He has an excellent sense of smell.

He can find missing people by
following the trail of their scent.

Aha! The dog finds the hiker
in a hole in the ground.

A rescue team helps the man out.

The dog saves the day!

Have you ever seen a horse dance?

Many horses are graceful.

But the **Lipizzan stallions**

(say: LI-pet-SAN)

perform in dancing shows.

Stallions are male horses.

Most Lipizzan stallions are born

brown or black and turn all white.

These Lipizzan leap, twirl,
and jump on their back legs.
Their riders wear fancy costumes
and tell them what steps to do.
These beautiful horses have been
dancing for 400 years.

Some horses had a really cool job

more than 100 years ago.

They delivered the mail!

Pony Express horses carried letters

way before e-mail and even trucks.

The Pony Express Trail went through

Missouri, Kansas, Nebraska, Wyoming,

Colorado, Utah, and Nevada,

and ended in California.

It was almost 2,000 miles long.

The horses and their riders
galloped all day and night.
They rode over prairies, plains,
deserts, and mountains.
But the Pony Express only lasted
two years, from 1860 to 1861.
Then the telegraph was made.
People could send messages faster
using this machine that sends signals.
So the Pony Express was stopped.

Chapter 4

Animals That Remember Things

Have you ever heard of

sending mail by pigeon post?

Carrier pigeons (say: PIH-jenz)

can take letters to people.

They are a type of homing pigeon.

This means they remember

the way to fly home by using

smells, sounds, and the sun.

These pigeons carried notes
in bottles tied around their legs.
They flew during wars to places
where the telegraph could not go.
This was a dangerous job.
One pigeon even won a medal
for being brave in battle!

The **scrub jay** is a busy bird.

At the end of summer,

it stores food for winter.

It picks thousands of acorns

and buries them one at a time.

Later, it remembers exactly where

the acorns are and digs them up.

What a brainy bird!

Some scientists also believe that
scrub jays can think carefully.
This scrub jay sees another bird
spying to see where it hides food.
Later, the scrub jay comes back
and moves its food to another spot.
It also ignores old food by knowing
how long the food has been hidden.
Scientists are still studying scrub jays
to see just how smart they are.

Can you find your way home?

Salmon (say: SAH-men) fish can.

Salmon are born in streams.

Then they grow bigger

and travel to the oceans.

They are one of the only fish that

live in both freshwater and saltwater.

Salmon swim thousands of miles

and then come back home.

This is called *migration*

(say: my-GRAY-shun).

Most salmon swim upstream

against the flow of water.

This is very hard to do.

Salmon do not eat anything

during their long migration.

These salmon leap up a waterfall.

They have found the stream

they were born in.

They are ready to lay eggs.

What an incredible trip home!

European eels are fish, but they look like slithery sea serpents. European eels migrate, too. They hatch in the Atlantic Ocean. Then they travel across the ocean to live in streams and rivers in Europe. A few years later, the eels migrate back to lay eggs.

These adult silver eels are
swimming out to the ocean.
They have big eyes and can
see well to swim at night.
They slide in the slippery mud
when the rivers dry up.
They are one of the only fish
that can move without water!

Emperor penguins mate for life.

They are excellent parents.

In winter the mother penguins

each lay one large egg.

Then the fathers hold the eggs

carefully on their feet for months

to keep them from freezing.

The mothers walk many miles
to the ocean to find food.
But they remember the way home.
They know to come back
as the eggs are about to hatch.
The mothers return, when it is
time for their babies to be born,
to feed and care for them.
They have great mom memory!

Elephants can do it all!

They communicate, use tools,

do jobs, and remember things.

Elephants talk to one another

by making low rumbling sounds

and trumpeting with their trunks.

Elephants do not have hands,

so they use their trunks as tools.

They also use tree branches to

swat flies and scratch itchy skin.

Asian elephants do lots of jobs.

They carry people, fix things,

and perform in the circus.

Elephants have great memories.

They remember places and things

by using their senses of smell and touch.

Elephants are totally amazing!

Animals may not be

as smart as people,

but they know many things

and help us in lots of ways.

We need all kinds of animals

for work, play, food, and love.

What far-out, furry friends

are your favorites?